friends · pajamas · bed · bathrobe · slippers · bath · soap

packages · cards · box · bread · honey · juice

apron · cookbook · cake tin · oven · presents · bicycle

engine · wheels · train · cake · candles

trees · flowers · cow · scarecrow · birds · butterflies · squirrels

spoons · napkins · balloons · party hats · sandwiches · cake · book

cards · bridge · horse · fence · tractor · tracks · toothbrush

A DORLING KINDERSLEY BOOK

Senior Art Editor Penny Britchfield
Senior Editor Sheila Hanly
Assistant Editor Finbar Hawkins
U.S. Assistant Editor Camela Decaire
Production Josie Alabaster

Photography Dave King
Additional photography Paul Bricknell and Alex Wilson

First American Edition, 1994
2 4 6 8 10 9 7 5 3 1

Published in the United States by
Dorling Kindersley Publishing, Inc., 95 Madison Avenue
New York, New York 10016

Library of Congress Cataloging-in-Publication Data

P.B. Bear's birthday party. — 1st American ed.
p.   cm.
Summary: P.B. the teddy bear celebrates his birthday with a cake,
a party for his friends, and lots of presents. Told in rebus form.
ISBN 1-56458-380-5
[1. Teddy bears—Fiction.   2. Birthdays—Fiction.   3. Rebuses.]
PZ7.T224 1994
[E]—dc20   93-29711
                                                      CIP
                                                      AC

Color reproduction by Colourscan
Printed in Italy

Acknowledgments
Dorling Kindersley would like to thank the following manufacturers
for permission to photograph copyright material:
The Manhattan Toy Company for "Antique Rabbit"
Folkmanis Inc. for "Furry Folk" hen puppet
Ty Inc. for "Toffee" the dog
Vera Small Designs for the lamb

Dorling Kindersley would also like to thank the following people
for their help in producing this book:
Jonathan Buckley, Hugh Sandys, Barbara Owen

 Can you find the
little bear in every scene?

P.B. BEAR'S

BIRTHDAY PARTY

Lee Davis

DK

DORLING KINDERSLEY

LONDON · NEW YORK · STUTTGART

Meet P.B. Bear.

The P. stands for Pajama, because his

are his favorite clothes.

 time is his favorite time of day.

Can you guess what the B. stands for?

One morning,  woke up early. This was

one day he didn't want to stay in .

He put on his  and and went into

the room. He filled the sink with water and

washed his face with . Then he dried his

fur with a and brushed it with a .

Finally he looked at himself in the .

"Happy birthday, ," he said to himself.

He put on his best , , and ,

and went downstairs.

8

There was a knock at the  .

"Mail for Mr. ," said the mailman, and he gave

two , three , and one

huge that was bigger than all the rest.

"I wonder what's in the ," said .

He wanted to open it right away, but he hadn't had

breakfast yet. So he went to the kitchen and ate some

and , and drank some .

Just as he was finishing, there was another knock at the .

There was his friend, Dermott the , with a

with a big on it.

10

"Happy birthday, ," said .

"Do you know what's in the big ?"

"I don't know," said .

"It's almost big enough for a , or a , or a ," said .

"It's so big, it might even be an !"

"We'll have to wait until I've opened it to find

out. But I've got some baking to do first.

Will you help me?" asked .

put on an and opened

a cook .

He put butter and sugar into a bowl and Dermott added the eggs and the flour. Then they took turns stirring the mixture with a spoon until it was smooth.

poured the mixture into a

and put it in the .

Just then there was another loud knock at the .

Look who had come to visit!

Russell the  brought a

wrapped in paper.

Hilda the brought a

wrapped in paper.

And Lucy the brought a

wrapped in paper.

"Happy birthday, !" they all shouted

as they handed him their .

"Thank you very much, everyone," said .

"What's in the big ?" asked .

"Maybe it's a ," said .

"Or a ," said .

"I know! It's a ," said .

"Why don't we open it and find out?" said .

got a pair of and

cut the .

He opened the .

What do you think he saw?

Inside the 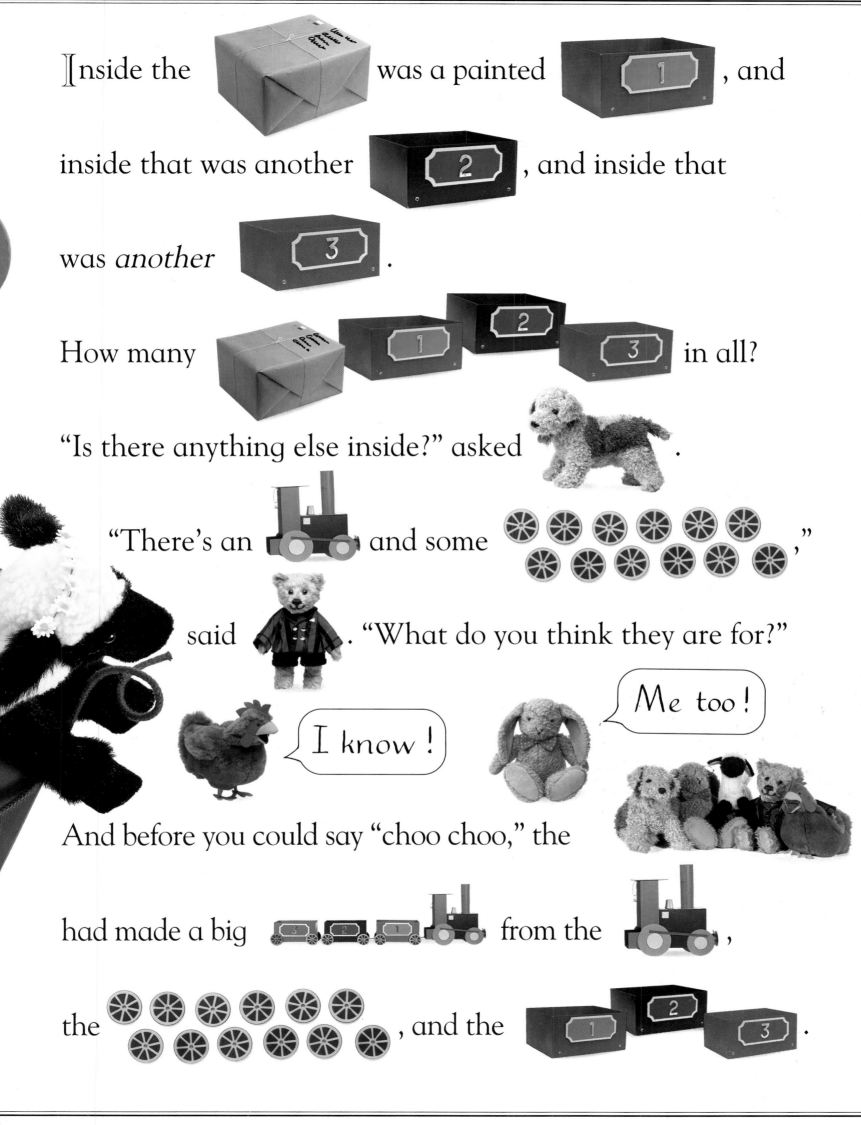 was a painted [box 1], and inside that was another [box 2], and inside that was *another* [box 3].

How many [box 1 2 3] in all?

"Is there anything else inside?" asked [dog].

"There's an [engine] and some [wheels]," said [bear]. "What do you think they are for?"

I know!

Me too!

And before you could say "choo choo," the [had] had made a big [train] from the [engine], the [wheels], and the [boxes 1 2 3].

"Let's go on a picnic!" said  . He

out of the . Then

while and the other

Can you see all the things

They put the in the

and the and

"All aboard!" they shouted as they

At last they were ready to leave.

rushed back to the kitchen to take the

 put icing and ||||| on the

 filled the [basket] .

they put in the [basket] ?

first car of the [train] ,

[letters] in the third car.

climbed into the second car.

"Off we go!" said [dog] .

The left and went out into . There were and and

"Ready or not,

closed his eyes and started to count.

"Boo! Happy birthday," Finally it stopped and they climbed out of the

the other

10 9 8 7 6 5 4 3 2 1

the

where there were

and

. It chugged past a

in the

. "Let's play hide and seek," said

who said, "Moo! Happy birthday,"

"I'll count to ten while you all hide."

here I come!" he shouted. Can you help

find

," and a

who said,

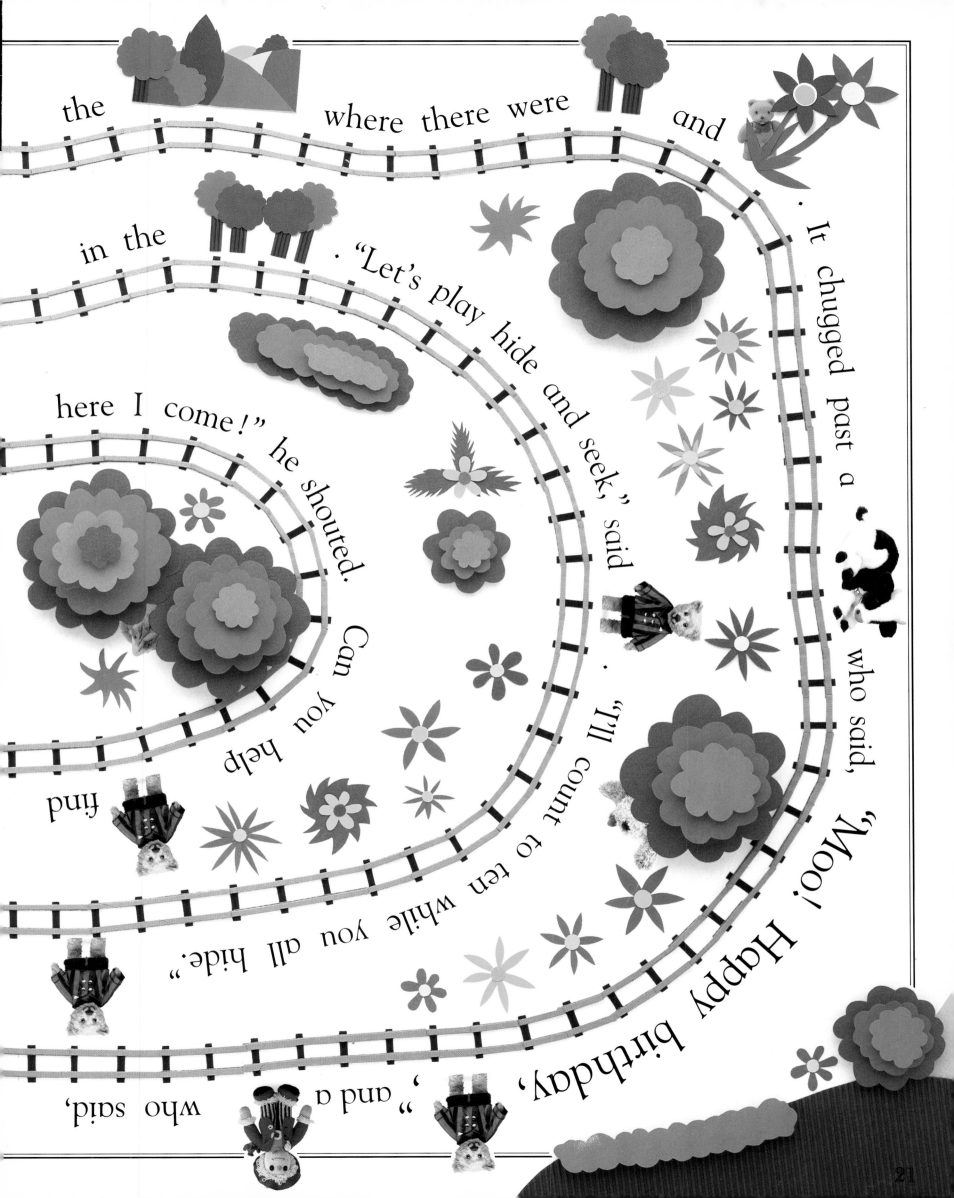

"Let's eat," said  .

"Good idea!" said the other . They took

the out and spread it on the ground.

Then they put out the , the ,

the , the , the , and the .

They blew up the and put on .

"Let's sing happy birthday to ," said

as he lit the on the .

Can you figure out how old is today?

The ate the tasty and drank

the . Then they all had a piece of .

22

Next it was time for [teddy bear] to open his [presents].

Which present would *you* open first?

Here is what he unwrapped: a [book], a [kite],

some [roller skates], a [puzzle], a [drum], and a [ball].

The [toys] wanted to play with the [presents].

[teddy bear], [lamb], and [rabbit] played a game

with the [ball]. [hen] tried out the [roller skates],

and [dog] flew the [kite].

It was time to go home. They packed up the  and

the and and in the third car.

"All aboard!"

The crossed a and went past a

for a that was driving very slowly across the .

and all the

put it in the first car of the [train] . They put

Only some crumbs were left behind for the [birds] .

shouted [dog]

who raced along the [gate] beside them. They had to stop

Soon the [train] was back in [town] .

said good-bye.

When he got home,  was very tired.

He took off his ⬛ , ⬛ , and ⬛ ,

and put on his ⬛ , his favorite clothes.

He brushed his teeth with his ⬛ .

Which of his ⬛ do you think

he took to ⬛ with him?

Good night, ⬛ !

P. B. Bear   Dermott   Russell   Lucy   Hilda

towel   brush   mirror   shorts   jacket   bow tie   door

present   bow   tiger   zebra   kangaroo   elephant

car   fire engine   scissors   string   boxes

cake   picnic basket   presents   town   country

tablecloth   plates   cups   knives   forks

kite   roller skates   jigsaw puzzle   drum   ball   presents